Pinterest Marketing in 2019 Made (Stupidly) Easy

Vol.4 of the "Small Business Marketing Made (Stupidly) Easy" Collection

by Michael Clarke

Founder, Punk Rock Marketing

Published in USA by: Punk Rock Marketing

Michael Clarke

© Copyright 2018

ISBN-13: 978-1-970119-13-8

Table of Contents

About the Author

Michael Clarke is a former cubicle monkey turned social media marketing consultant and author.

He is also the owner of the world's most neurotic Jack Russell Terrier.

Also By Michael Clarke

TWITTER MARKETING IN 2019 MADE
(STUPIDLY) EASY

VIDEO MARKETING IN 2019 MADE
STUPIDLY EASY

FACEBOOK MARKETING IN 2019 MADE
STUPIDLY EASY

INSTAGRAM MARKETING IN 2019 MADE
STUPIDLY EASY

LINKEDIN MARKETING IN 2019 MADE
STUPIDLY EASY

EMAIL MARKETING IN 2019 MADE
STUPIDLY EASY

SEARCH ENGINE OPTIMIZATION IN
2019 MADE STUPIDLY EASY

A Special FREE Gift for You!

If you'd like FREE instant access to my seminar "How to Make a Damn Good Living With Social Media (Even If You Hate Social Media" then head over to **PunkRockMarketing.com/Free**. (What else you gonna do? Watch another "Twilight" movie?!)

Prologue: How I Stopped Hating Pinterest (and Started Making Money)

I used to think Pinterest was the Lady Gaga of social networks. (Without the dress shaped like an egg.)

That even though Pinterest was hip and popular and visually engaging and was giving us a glimpse of what users would want to consume in the **future...**

It was also something that wasn't designed for ME. (I don't sell Prada purses or kitchen cabinet installations.)

But then the strangest thing in the world happened - I made MONEY with Pinterest.

Real money. (With little effort.)

That's because:

- Pinterest users GLADLY share advertorial images of products and services (with the price tag attached!)
- Pinterest delivers more referring website traffic than LinkedIn, YouTube and Tumblr COMBINED…
- Pinterest users BUY more often than users of other social networks. (And when they buy, they spend a hell of a lot more money than Facebookers and Twitterers combined.)

And though I was resistant at first - like being dragged to "Bath and Body Works" by my wife - I swallowed my pride, and my inherent distrust of yoga photos, and jumped into the swirling vortex of Pinterest.

And, I made EVERY mistake a Pinterest marketer can make. (Most of which I will help you try to avoid.)

But, gradually, I started to NOT suck so badly. And what I found was a-stounding. Pinterest didn't just boost my traffic. It:

- Increased my sales
- Boosted my email subscriber counts
- Reduced product return rates
- Cut down on customer support costs
- Put me in contact with affiliates and JV partners
- Created more leads (and more customers) than Facebook and Twitter

And that's when it occurred to me: Pinterest's appeal isn't just pretty photos accumulated in a virtual scrapbook.

Pinterest allows people to ORGANIZE their world.

To put their life experience into themed boards that shows their friends — and the rest of the Pinterest universe — who they REALLY are. (Or perhaps who they'd desperately like to be.)

Unlike a Facebook page, which can have a multitude of voices and rants and complaints (all without any context to one other)...

...or a Twitter feed, which is like drinking from a 140-character social media fire hose...

...or YouTube which is like visiting the cantina from Star Wars. (Who knows what you'll find in there?)

A *Pinterest board*, such as the popular Nordstrom "Shoe Lust" board with its 156K followers, is about as simple as it gets.

It's about pictures of pretty shoes. That's it.

It's not about users or profiles or friends or retweets or likes or RSS feeds or blog posts or anything that feels like homework...

...it's about a single place where people share pictures of a SPECIFIC thing, such as triathlon exercises, DIY bathroom ideas, Indian curry recipes...whatever.

And having something in our lives that simple, focused, fun, and ultra-visual (meaning we can consume it in a matter of a few seconds) provides real benefit to people living in a smartphone-infused world.

And if we as marketers can tell a simple STORY about our products and services, that connects to people on a primal, emotional level...

Then not only will we **sell more stuff,** but we'll be helping our customers connect to that magical, inspirational, kick-ass part of themselves.

And doing that can impact your business, and the world, in ways you can't imagine.

Still skeptical?

Think I'm full of Pinterest bull crap? That's okay.

I would have thought I was full of it too. (Nothing changes one's mind like adding commas to a bank balance.)

So...let's enroll in the department of Pinterest studies and go make you some moo-lah!

Chapter 1:

Pinterest Made Super Simple

"The best way to predict the future is to create it."
-Peter Drucker

Before we jump into the deep end of the Pinterest pool, I want to make sure we're all on the same page. (Nothing more confusing in this world than a social network and all its oddly named components.)

So, if you feel you got a good handle on what Pinterest is, but you just want to start crushing it from a marketing side, then jump over to Chapter 2.

But if you're relatively new to Pinterest, and don't know your pinboard from your repin, then up

your Pinterest IQ with these answers to these
Pinterest FAQs:

Pinterest FAQ No.1: How the Hell Do I Make Money With Pinterest?

How do we turn all these pins and repins and
likes and pinboards into hard currency?

Most social networks FROWN on overt selling.
(Just see how many times you link out to your sales
pages on Facebook before you incur a "fan" revolt.)

But Pinterest is different. For one thing, the
entire Pinterest ecosystem is based on people pinning
pictures of:

- Stuff They Want
- Stuff That Represents Their Style
- Stuff That Inspires Them

Market your stuff in a way that touches on one,
if not all of those, and you have something that
doesn't "feel" like marketing.

Best of all, Pinterest users ARE buyers. They want to spend money on cool stuff.

And studies show they spend a ton more than any other social network user. (Nearly double what Facebook and Twitter users spend, combined.)

And if your cool stuff is aligned with their themed pinboards, and the boards of their friends, then you will find a new source of leads who not only share your content and follow your company…but they also **buy your stuff**.

The important thing is you GOTTA tell a story with your product or service. You know, besides, "We sell stuff, so we can make money."

Come up with a compelling WHY for your company — "We're an organic diaper company who believes in a no-chemical childhood…" "We're a group of accountants who wear blue jeans and motorcycle jackets to work…" — and you're 75% of the way there with your Pinterest marketing.

Pinterest FAQ No. 2: Yeah, But What If I Don't Sell to Women?

There's no getting around this: 65% of all Pinterest users are women.

But maybe that's not a bad thing.

According to She-Conomy, women represent nearly two-thirds of all consumer spending. (That means whether your product or service is for men OR women, chances are women will end up buying it at some point.)

Now, if you're selling a product or service that absolutely no woman would ever want to look at (or even imagine thinking about it) — such as a seduction dating information product or a Hooter's video series — then think seriously before plunging forward with your Pinterest marketing strategy.

This doesn't mean, though, you can't sell products *designed for men*.

As any advertising expert will tell you: Old Spice's ingenious "The Man Your Man Could Smell

Like" campaigns were NOT intended for men. They were designed for my wife. Guess what I'm using for deodorant now.

Pinterest FAQ No.3: What's a Pin?

A pin is simply an image or video that users add to their Pinterest profile. Somewhat like the Pinterest version of the "tweet" or the Facebook "status update."

That's it. Don't over-think it.

Pinterest FAQ No.4: How Do I Pin?

There are four different ways to pin something:

- Clicking the "Pin It" button on a website page.
- Clicking on your Pinterest bookmarklet in your browser.
- Adding the website URL in the "Add From a Website" field of your Pinterest

dashboard.

- Upload an image or video directly to Pinterest.

All pins link back to their original source. (No matter how many times they are shared.)

Pinterest FAQ No.5: What Do I Put Into My Pin?

We're going to cover this in some detail in Chapter 5, but for now just know that when you "pin" something there are three things to consider:

- What specific image or video on a web page the pin will feature.
- What specific pinboard the pin is associated to.
- What's in the text description of the pin. Example: Caption, links, calls-to-action, etc.

Again, this is vital marketer real estate. In Chapter 5, we'll go over the whats and hows of the perfect pin to help you reach your marketing goals.

Pinterest FAQ No.6: Okay, So What's a Pinboard?

Pinboards, or boards, are themed collections of pins. They're kind of like mini-Facebook pages, but without all the Mafia Wars invites.

The whole concept of the pinboard can be confusing the first time out. Just know:

- Each pin is associated to a specific pinboard
- You can create as many pinboards as you want
- Followers of yours can follow either your entire profile, which means they get updated on everything you do, or they can follow specific, individual boards.

Pinterest FAQ No.7: What Should I Create Pinboards About?

Almost anything you want!

As long as you don't go with what Pinterest gives you out of the box. As a Pinterest user, you are given a few default boards upon signing up. They are called "My Styles" and "Places and Spaces."

These need to be changed immediately. These are horrible names for anything, let alone a Pinterest board.

You can organize a board around almost anything:

- A theme
- An event
- A special promotion
- A product or service
- Your customers (or a segment of your customers)
- Testimonials
- Quotes

- A special private board that only invited users can contribute to
- …anything!

And in Chapter 4, I go into a ton more detail on the best practices for creating boards.

Pinterest FAQ No.8: Is a Repin the Same Thing as a Pin

Repins are like retweets. **Sorta**.

Like retweets, a Pinterest user finds an interesting pin they think is cool. They then repin it to one of their "boards." The original pinner still retains credit for the pin, no matter how many times it is repinned.

Nearly 80% of all the activity on Pinterest is *repins*. They are an important part of your Pinterest strategy, but to separate yourself from the Pinterest pack you'll need to do more pinning than repinning.

Pinterest FAQ No.9: What's a Like? Is it Like a "Facebook Like"?

Yeah, kinda.

When you "like" a specific pin, it is added to your profile's collection of "likes." (I suppose for those folks who feel that the four seconds it takes to "repin" something is far more than they're willing to spend.)

"Likes" are not added to a user's particular pinboard but are instead added to a user's "likes" page. (This is more of a social vote, than a traffic-getting strategy.)

To "like" a pin, simply hover over the pin and "click" on the HEART icon.

Pinterest FAQ No.10: How Do I Make Sure I Don't Waste My Time With Pinterest?

Well, you're reading this book, aren't ya? :)

Seriously, here's a minimum-effort strategy I'd like you to think about before crashing the Pinterest party.

Can you or somebody on your team commit to:

- Pinning 5-20 pins a day? Remember each of these take about three seconds. (That's almost a full minute's work.)
- Following 25-50 other Pinterest users per day?
- Creating 10-20 boards for different themes and topics relates to your business? (Just need these to get up and running.)
- Throwing an occasional contest to boost your fan base and increase your amount of leads?
- Adding pretty pictures to the web content you produce?

If you can do that, and it seriously shouldn't take you more than 10 minutes a day, you will be light years ahead of 92% of the businesses out there on Pinterest. (And you'll be making a hell of a lot more money than them too.)

Chapter 2:

4 Steps to a Kick-Ass Pinterest Profile

"If you have nothing to create at all, then perhaps you create yourself."
-C.G. Jung

Before we jump into the creation of your fabulous Pinterest boards and grow your Pinterest follower base (and make some serious money from our new Pinterest efforts) we need to create one seriously kick-ass Pinterest profile.

Because a Pinterest account isn't just where your pins and pinboards live, it's also a huge source of referral website traffic. (And that traffic is especially effective when sent to opt-in pages and sales pages.)

And don't forget your Pinterest profile provides a serious SEO boost to whatever external location it links to. (Way bigger than your Facebook or Twitter profiles ever will.)

So here are my FOUR Kick-Ass Steps to Creating an Awesome Pinterest Profile to get you primed for domination:

Kick-Ass Pinterest Profile Step No.1: Create a Business Account

Just like with the Facebook universe, there are two kinds of profiles for Pinterest: personal and business.

We want the business.

Not just for the obvious reason — that we are, in fact, doing business-y things. But there are basic, though important, reasons for having a business account:

- Promoting your wares on a personal account violates Pinterest's terms of service. (And could get your account banned.)

- You can designate your business name as the profile name for a business account. Sounds obvious, but this is not something you can do with a personal account, in which you have to have a regular (first name, surname) naming structure.

- As of the writing of this book, Pinterest will plan to add some new features for business accounts down the line. (My guess? Cool analytics and more creative profile display options. But then again…I thought Cyndi Lauper would be a way bigger success than Madonna. So what'dya I know?)

So how do you set up your business account? Here's how:

- **Go to the dedicated Pinterest business page**. You can find it at: http://business.pinterest.com.

- **Click "Join as a Business."**

- **Fill out the key info**. Make sure your company name hasn't already been taken by somebody else. (It happens.)

- **Add a keyword in the username if you can**. It's not required: but the username carries a HUGE SEO boost to your profile. (Meaning your Pinterest boards could eventually show up in Google rankings for important keywords.)

- **Verify your website.** Huh? Verify your website? What the heck does that mean? Well, funny you should ask, because…

Kick-Ass Pinterest Profile Step No.2: Verify Your Website

You'd think this would be easy. You'd be wrong.

Pinterest requires all business accounts be "verified" by having the user place code on their website or blog. (Check Out

Yeah! Code! Sounds fun, doesn't it?

You can do this two different ways:

1. By uploading an HTML file (generated by Pinterest) to your website's server

2. By adding a meta tag (generated by Pinterest) to your website's home page

If what I said sounds like I'm speaking Klingon, then I'd like to make recommendation: Head over to a site like Fiverr.com and pay the five bucks to have somebody do it for you. For somebody who knows what they're doing, it'll take five minutes. For us technically challenged schlubs…who knows?

If you know your way around FTP and the back-end of your blog, head over to http://punkrockmarketing.com/pinterestverify. There, I've got some detailed instructions on how to do it.

Again, if you're not sure, hire a professional. (Or that precocious 12-year-old cousin of yours who seems to know everything.)

Kick-Ass Pinterest Profile Step No.3: Create an "About Me" Section That Doesn't Suck

This is where a lot of Pinterest marketers totally screw up.

The "about me" section of your Pinterest profile is valuable real estate. And shouldn't be wasted on some rambling pointless dissertation of what kind of DIY bathroom project you're into or your favorite flavor of homemade incense.

In the "About Me" section you can:

- **Talk about the benefits of your company's products or services.** Remember: People care about benefits, not features.
- **Add in appropriate keywords.** If

you're not sure which keywords are the best, head over to http://punkrockmarketing.com/keywordtool. I've got a step-by-step process on a FREE resource to help you out.

- **If you're a local business, USE geo-targeted keywords.** Not abbreviations; good, old spelled-out cities.

- **Put in your email.** Unless you don't want people to email you, which you might not.

- **Link to a landing page other than your home page.** Such as a place to collect email addresses. (You are collecting email addresses, aren't you?)

Kick-Ass Pinterest Profile Step No.4: One Killer Profile Image to Rule Them All

Ya wouldn't think this would make a difference.

You'd be wrong.

Pinterest is all about pictures and nowhere is that more evident than with your Pinterest profile image.

Here's what you need to know about profile images:

1. **The image should be square.** Pinterest recommends an upload size of 600 pixels by 600 pixels to allow for the highest amount of resolution. (And if that's what they recommend, that's probably what we should do.)

2. **The image should focus on one subject.** The picture will be resized to 165 pixels by 165 pixels and group shots can look muddled at that size. (So can vague, indeterminate nature shots.)

3. **People shots are best if they're crisp.** No blurry, fuzzy iPhone shots you took in the dark holding a margarita...err...I mean a library book.

4. **The image should evoke a "feeling" that**

relates somehow to your company. This can be loosely defined but go for whatever positive feeling you'd like associated with your product and website. (Whether it's a rainbow, or your CEO. Or your CEO standing in front of a rainbow!)

5. **Avoid logos, unless they're awesome.** I don't like logos used as profile images. (Think they appear too artificial.) But if you got a killer one, then use it.

6. **The name of the image should contain your company name.** Not "IMG_1" or "Pinterest_Logo," but instead "ABC-Accounting" or "Joe's-Pool-Cleaning." This will give your Pinterest account some extra SEO juice.

Chapter Two Key Takeaways:

- **Create a Pinterest business account.** (It'll make your life much easier.)

- **Verify your website.** If you're tech-y, you can upload an HTML file or meta tag to your website. If not, hire somebody to do it for you.

- **Fill up the "about me" section of your profile with goodies.** Add keywords, links and benefits of your business in this valuable part of your profile.

- **Find a great profile image** that is: 600 x 600 pixels, features one subject, shows people (or a great logo) and has your company name in the file name.

Chapter 3: 7 Tools Every Pinterest Marketer Must Have

"If all you have is a hammer in the toolbox, everything looks like a nail."

-Bernard Baruch

Okay, here's where we separate from the pack.

Here's where we stand out from the rest of the Pinterest hobbyists and flex some serious Pinterest marketing muscle.

Most of the tools I advocate below are 100% FREE. (And my favorite tool of all costs less than a couple of bucks a month.)

But no joke…adding these tools to your Pinterest marketing arsenal will make it SO MUCH

EASIER to attract new leads and find those elusive, paying customers.

So, here are my SEVEN Must-Have Pinterest Tools to get you ready for maximum Pinterest marketing supremacy:

Must-Have Pinterest Tool No.1: A Camera That Doesn't Royally Suck

Nothing sells a product on Pinterest like a kick-ass photo. And chances are you already have a decent well-stocked camera sitting in your pocket.

That's right. Your smartphone!

Most smartphones made in the last couple of years pack plenty of camera-taking punch to suit your needs. (If you know how to use it right.)

Here are a few quicks tips when taking photos with your smartphone:

- **Turn the phone sideways.** This gives you more photo-editing area to work with later. Nothing screams "amateur" like a vertical smartphone photo.
- **Tap on the screen to indicate the**

subject of the picture before hitting "click." This lets the phone do all kinds of auto-focus and stabilization stuff that'll make your photo sing.

- **Lean against a wall or some kind of flat surface.** This avoids needless movement which can affect crispness and photo clarity.

And what do ya do if you don't have a smartphone?

Well, for just a couple hundred dollars you could buy something from the very under-rated and high-performing Canon PowerShot series.

You could spend a lot more on a Digital SLR camera. But if that's the case, you don't need my camera-buying tips.

No matter what your camera of choice, here are a couple of general tips when shooting people or products:

- **Shoot outside if you can.** Natural light is always better than artificial light.

- **Late mornings** (8:30 a.m. - 10:00 a.m.) and **late afternoons** (4:00 p.m. - 6:00 p.m.) are "magic" times to shoot photos because the lighting is warm. Noontime is the worst, it makes people look like vampires.

- **"Don't look into the light!"** Always try to shoot with the sun to your back.

- **Keep the light even**. If shooting inside, try to keep the light source behind you consistent on all sides. (You can buy desk lamps and clip them behind you, if needed.)

Must-Have Pinterest Tool No. 2: Free (and Legal) Sources for Photos

Not all the images you share on Pinterest are gonna be ones that came from your camera.

(Nobody wants to look at your product pics all day. Secondly, you gotta a frickin' business to run.)

That's why it's crucial to find sources for FREE (and legal) photos you can use under the Creative Commons license.

Note: Creative Commons has a wide variety of rights distinctions. It's worth learning about. Just head over to: http://en.wikipedia.org/wiki/Creative_Commons to get more information about it.

The LEGAL part of "Legal and Free" is important. You don't want to just grab pics from Google Images. It's wrong and could get you thrown into a Bulgarian work camp.

Here are some of my favorite places to grab open-source photos: (Note: Be sure to check the copyright on all images before using)

- Flickr (http://flickr.com)
- Morgue File (http://morguefile.com)
- PixaBay (https://pixabay.com/)

And when you're on the look-out for photos remember:

- **You gotta GRAB people.** You want crisp, sharp photos...that stand out! Better to be shocking than boring.
- **Forget pretty, go with real.** Stock photos of supermodels doing "ordinary" things look staged and really DUMB.
- **Go with your gut.** Find photos that evoke a "feeling," don't just look for photos that make literal sense.

Must-Have Pinterest Tool No.3: PicMonkey

The cool thing about photo-editing tools, such as the supremely awesome **PicMonkey**, is it makes you look like a much better photographer than you actually are. (As a very mediocre photographer myself, this is a great asset.)

Now, you don't HAVE to use PicMonkey. You could use FREE tools such as Gimp, or expensive tools like Photoshop.

But PicMonkey is my secret Pinterest marketing weapon because it's:

- Cheap — they have a FREE option and a very reasonable paid option.
- Easy to Use
- Powerful — lets you correct lighting issues and offers a TON of out-of-the-box effects perfect for making your photos POP.
- Made for non-techie folks (like me).
- Lets you add a company watermark to your images

But I think the BIGGEST benefit PicMonkey gives you is the ability to add a text overlay to your photos.

This is HUGE. With a text overlay you can:

- Add quotes to images. Wanna create a

viral meme? Just put a quote over a pretty picture.

- Ask people to visit your website.
- Ask people to "pin" a photo.
- Suggest people sign up for your email list to get that FREE THING you're giving away.

And the crazy thing is: just asking people to "pin" your photo increases engagement by 80%.

I know. It shouldn't be that easy. Telling people you want them to do something…then having them do it.

But it can be! And PicMonkey is in, my never humble opinion, the best friend a Pinterest marketer can have.

Must-Have Pinterest Tool No.4: Pictures (and Lots of 'Em) on Your Website

This one isn't so much a tool as it is a best

practice.

If you aren't already adding a picture to every piece of content you publish on your site — whether it be a blog post, essay, FAQ, About page, deranged manifesto about the government, etc. — then you are missing out on a huge source of Pinterest traffic.

We've touched briefly on what KIND of photos to look for. (Crisp, interesting, no supermodels using laundry detergent.) But here's what you need to know before uploading actual photos to your site:

- **"Name" the photo with a keyword**. For instance, if the blog post is about "How to Make Decorative Candles," then a great picture name would be: "Decorative_Candles," not "Photo1."

- **Get in fast**. Try to get the photo in the first couple paragraphs of your blog post or webpage.

- **Caption this!** If you have room for a caption, be sure to include a keyword there.

Must-Have Pinterest Tool No.5: Pinterest Buttons…Everywhere!

Pinterest buttons let you leverage the existing website and blog traffic you are already getting to your site and encourages those visitors to pin your existing content. (Now you know WHY it's so important to make sure all your groovy content is adorned with killer images.)

Creating the button is simple; it's just a matter of generating code you throw onto your site.

To do this, head over to http://punkrockmarketing.com/pinterestbutton to generate the code. You'll find a couple of design and text options. Nothing super fancy here, but it'll get the job done.

There are two important types of buttons to focus on:

a. **The Pin It Button:** This lets folks pin a photo located on a specific web page to the pin board of their choosing.

b. **The "Follow" Button:** This lets people "follow" you on Pinterest.

So where do we put these buttons?

Here's how I use them:

"PIN IT" BUTTON

- In the body of a blog post
- The sidebar of a website
- The header of a website
- The footer of every blog post
- Next to every video

"FOLLOW ON PINTEREST" BUTTON

- The "Thank You for Subscribing" page
- The checkout page
- The email signature
- The message board profile signatures
- The website footer

And if that sound super complicated - or

something reserved for people with a Ph.D. in Internet engineering - then just hire your designer or local unemployed fifteen-year-old to help you out.

Must-Have Pinterest Tool No.6: Get a Pinterest Bookmarklet

I know. I hate the term bookmarklet too. (Offends my English-Major sensibilities.) But they're huge Pinterest time-savers.

Basically a "bookmarklet" is an extension you install on your web browser of choice that lets you "pin" things to your Pinterest profile with the simple click of a button. (Told ya Pinterest takes way less time than other social networks.)

To set up the bookmarklet, just head over to http://about.pinterest.com/goodies/ and you can grab the bookmarklet thing-y. (You can even get the Pinterest smartphone app there.)

Must-Have Pinterest Tool No.7: Put a Board Widget on Your Website

Before you say: "What the hell is a board widget? And why should I care?…"

…a board widget is a piece of code you throw onto your website that shows your website visitors the latest pins from your Pinterest account.

Another good reason to separate personal from business with your Pinterest activities.

Now, in the early days of your Pinterest career, this widget will look a little skimpy. But before you know it, you'll have a robust Pinterest offering.

And what better way to show off your Pinterest efforts and "spice" up your website, visually, than adding a little board widget action?

To generate the code, just head over to that same location I mentioned earlier (http://punkrockmarketing.com/pinterestbutton) to get your board widget created and your website looking somewhat less sucky.

Chapter Three Key Takeaways:

- **Make sure you have a halfway decent camera.** You don't need a full-on DSLR, your smartphone will most likely work.

- **Shoot outside, if possible.** And always keep the camera steady, with the light to your back.

- **Find free photos, legally.** Great places to find free (legal) photos are PixaBay, MorgueFile and Flickr. (Be sure to check on the rights of every photo you use.)

- **Get awesome photos with PicMonkey.** Be sure to add text overlays that encourage folks to "pin" your photos.

- **Go photo crazy.** Include a crisp, interesting photo with every piece of content you publish on your site.

- **Add Pinterest buttons — both "Pin It" buttons and "Follow Me" buttons — everywhere on your site.** That includes headers, footers, sidebars, thank you pages and in the body of all your content.

- **Grab the Pinterest bookmarklet** to save you a bunch of time.

- **Place a board widget on your site**, especially if your site needs sprucing up.

Chapter 4:

The Marvelous & Fantastic World of PinBoards

"Great works are performed not by strength but by perseverance."

-Samuel Johnson

This chapter will blow your mind.

Seriously, when you discover some of the cool, awesome things you can do with Pinboards you might just need hospitalization from your instant Pinterest awesomeness.

While it's true most casual users experience Pinterest through the pins they use to tag whatever catches their eye…it's really the BOARDS where we find our biggest marketing potential.

Because Pinboards are like little silos of super-focused, ultra-targeted awesomeness that let users check out our products, share our content and eventually buy our stuff.

Earlier I said, unlike its social-media cohort Facebook, a Pinterest user does not follow EVERY single thing you do on Pinterest.

That means users can just "follow" and check out the things they want.

Example: A user can "follow" a Nordstrom board dedicated to Prada shoes, without having to follow the "Coach handbag" board, which they may or may not have any interest in.

And it means you can meet your prospective customers in a huge variety of ways. (And sell them a huge variety of products and services.)

So, now you've got the 411 of how Pinterest boards work, let's show you how to plan, create and fill those boards with awesome money-making content.

And we'll do that with my THREE Step Blueprint to a Kick-Ass Pinterest Board:

Kick-Ass Blueprint Step No.1: Realize What's Possible

I used to think Pinterest boards were just a place to house all my product photos and affiliate crap.

Boy, was I wrong.

There is (virtually) no limit to the things you can do with Pinterest boards. There are a couple of obvious ones:

- Create a board for each different product or service you offer in your business.
- Create a board where customers can give you feedback on your products.
- Create a board where customers can find out about any big company news or future product launches.

- And that's all nice. But it doesn't EVEN scratch the surface. Because you can do things like create:

- A testimonial board for your products where followers and customers can leave comments.

- A board highlighting members of your company. (People LOVE these.)

- A board showing behind-the-scenes stuff about your company. Videos work great here.

- A board promoting and recapping a live event.

- A board that offers how-to advice on a specific topic. (Lowe's does a great job of this with their DIY boards.)

- A board that offers supplemental training. (This can work great for info-product creators and those in the educational space.)

- A board that spotlights some of your

top clients or customers. (You can imagine some of the goodwill this might create.)

- A board specifically for affiliates.
- A board for virtually any special offer, coupon, contest, promotion, or product you've got in the works.

The possibilities are endless. If you've got rich media (photos, video, audio) that can be themed and organized…then putting them into a board is a no-brainer idea.

Kick-Ass Blueprint Step No.2: Come Up With a Board Plan

Now you've got some idea of what you COULD create, it's time to figure out what you SHOULD make.

Not all the boards I mentioned earlier will apply to your business. And that's okay.

What you want to do is be daring. Come up with

interesting, creative ways you can show off your company and its offerings.

Here are a couple of questions to get you started:

- How many **products and services** does my business have?

- Do we have **happy customers/clients** we'd like to spotlight?

- Are there certain **areas of expertise** where we could be a resource to potential customers?

- What would be the best way to **break up these areas of expertise** into separate boards? (Again, Lowe's does this really well: breaking up the DIY boards by project.)

- Do we have upcoming **events** that would make for cool boards? (If so, make damn sure SOMEBODY takes a lot of photos and video.)

- Do we have any **future product launches** or new services that could use a board?

- What would be a cool, interesting way to **feature our team**? (Videos? Blog posts? Pictures of our employees' pets?)

Try to shoot for at least 10 or so boards that could house at least 25-50 pins apiece. This will be enough to get you started and help your Pinterest account look thriving and robust.

Kick-Ass Blueprint Step No.3: Create Your Boards (and Give 'Em Non-Sucky Names)

Okay, so now you got a plan! It's time to dig in and create your boards.

The HOW is pretty simple. You just:

- Click the Add+ button in the upper right-hand corner of your Pinterest home page.
- Select the "Create a Board" option.

- Enter the name, category, and (any) contributors to the board…then click "Create Board."

But there's a couple important things to keep in mind when creating your boards:

- **Try to get a keyword in if you can**. Your SEO ranking will thank you for it.

- **Put a twist at the end** to give your board name personality. Instead of "Marketing Tips," you could do: a) "Marketing Tips From Andy" or "Marketing Tips From the Lab" or the very simple "Marketing Tips That Don't Suck."

- **You CAN change the name of your board later.** BUT changing the name changes the URL. So if you have links to that board, it may break those links.

- **Don't stress the "category" choice** too much. Pinterest doesn't give you a lot of options. And most of the ones they give you are boring.

- **Add contributors**, if relevant. Pinterest boards can create some cool micro-communities. So if it's part of the board plan, specify here who can contribute to your board.

Chapter Four Key Takeaways:

- **There are TONS of different ways you can theme and organize your Pinterest boards.** My personal favorites include: 1) Highlighting customers 2) Collecting testimonials 3) Employee spotlights 4) How-to resources 5) Affiliate boards and 6) Future product launches.

- **Brainstorm different boards that might work for your business.** Anything that tells a "story" with pictures and video would work.

- **Be sure to include keywords in your board names.** And add "spice" at the end to stand out from the pack.

Chapter 5:

6 Keys to Creating the Perfect Pin

"Bite off more than you can chew, then chew it."
-Courage Wolf

Ah, yes. Pins.

The raw currency that makes the Pinterest economy go.

Pins aren't like Facebook status updates and tweets. For one thing they last forever. As opposed to tweets and Facebook updates, which seem to have the half-life of a nanosecond.

And pins aren't a "vote" for something a user likes. Such as a Facebook "like" or "retweet."

When somebody "pins" a photo, they decide which "board" that "pin" will live in. And that "pin" becomes a part of their board ecosystem, not just something to fill their newsfeed.

So, offering compelling and interesting content that people will "pin" and "repin" is our primary job as Pinterest marketing gurus.

And filling our boards with pin-worthy goodies is an important first step to attracting followers and building up our Pinterest street cred.

So, that's what we will do.

In this chapter I will show you my SIX Keys to the Perfect Pin. But first let's go over the mechanics. How do we actually "pin" and "repin" stuff the RIGHT way?

How Pinning Works

1. **You decide on something to pin.** Either through uploading a photo or video, using

your bookmarklet browser extension, clicking on a web location's "pin it" button or pasting the URL directly into your Pinterest dashboard.

2. You choose **which of your boards** the pin will live in.

3. **Fill out the pin's description**…and you're done!

How Repinning Works

This is even simpler. You find a "pin" somebody else has already shared on Pinterest and:

1. Hover over the pin and click "Pin It"

2. Select which board you want to add the repin to

3. Click "Pin It"

As my 15-year-old emo cousin would say: "It ain't rocket surgery."

What You Should Fill Your Boards With

This is really the big question facing us as marketers. How much NEW, original pinning do we do?

And how much repinning (or using other people's content) should we do? Especially since repinning is a great way to grab new followers. (More on that in the next chapter.)

If it's a board focused on internal/company stuff — such as an "employee spotlight" board or a "client appreciation" board — then obviously the pins associated with that board will be limited in scope. And repinning will play less of a role.

Although, when appropriate, opening up the board to outside contributors can lead to some interesting content you hadn't thought of being shared on the board.

But if it's a board that is about a more general theme or area of expertise — such as a "DIY

Bathroom Project" board — I like to keep the mix of pins somewhere in the neighborhood of:

- 50% repins
- 25% pins of other resources (Such as blog posts, YouTube videos, anything I didn't create)
- 25% featuring my own company's blog posts, images, videos, and photos.

Now you may NOT have enough visual content to fill up that 25%. And that's okay. Do what you can.

Just commit you and your team to creating more visual content — could be as simple as putting an inspirational quote on a pretty picture — from here on out.

All right, enough of the jibber-jabber...let's get to the 6 Keys to the Perfect Pin!

Perfect Pin Key No.1: Find Cool Stuff to Pin

This will depend on the specific board you are pinning items to, but here's the stuff that's worked best for me:

- **Inspirational quotes** over pretty pictures. (This NEVER fails.)
- **Product stills.** Make sure they are crisp and non-sucky.
- **Photos and videos of my team** doing human, non-sales-y things.
- **How-to videos.** Both that we created and curated from somewhere else.
- **Infographics.** If you want resources on how to create your own FREE infographic, check out http://punkrockmarketing.com/infographic.
- **Funny videos and pictures.** If you can get an animal in there, even better.

- **Checklists, insider guides, cheat sheets.** Anything that smells like a resource.
- **Repins of other Pinterest users** that fit in with the theme of your board.

And where do you find these assets?

Well here are some of my favorite go-to spots:

- **PopUrls:** This "best of" collection of the stuff that's viral and popular on the Internet is my browser home page. (You'll find a broad range of content here, from the profane to the scholarly erudite.) Poke around and you might just find the perfect stuff to add to your Pinterest stew.
- **AllTop:** This is a site that collects the best blog posts on the web about a topic. And it's done by humans! Check it out, there's virtually a page about everything here.

- **Photo of the Day:** There are tons of Photo of the Day sites. Pick one that fits your business and use it to fill up your Pinterest archive.

- **Google Alerts:** This tool allows you to set up alerts, based on keywords, that will have ALL of the latest blog posts, news stories, discussions, etc., about that topic delivered to your inbox.

I like to create a Google Doc where my team and I can throw in URLs for interesting visual stuff we come across during of our workday. (You'll be shocked how quickly your Pinterest reserves can fill up.)

The key thing is to mix it up. Don't pin everything you see from The New York Times and The Daily Beast. Keep it varied.

Perfect Pin Key No.2: Decide Best Time to Pin

This is not written in stone.

But according to Reachli, a Pinterest analytics company, the best times to post on Pinterest are between 2:00 p.m. - 4:00 p.m. EST and again from 8:00 p.m. - 1:00 a.m. EST.

And I have to agree.

Pinterest is definitely an afternoon after-work activity. So experiment with your posting times, but late afternoon and evening definitely seem to work best. If you're a local business, start with evenings and work backwards to find your pinning sweet spot.

Perfect Pin Key No.3: Gather Great Imagery

Doesn't matter whether your pin should promote a new blog post or the fact you made squash soup for the first time, making sure you have good, eye-catching imagery is VITAL to your Pinterest success.

But what makes an image good? And eye-catching?

Well, I'm no photo creative expert, but here are a couple things that the data has shown:

- **Think "lifestyle" first** - No matter what you're hawking ask yourself: "Does this image sell an ideal lifestyle?" Pinterest is creative and aspirational; it should not feel like homework. So, make sure your imagery captures the mood you want.

- **Light over dark** - Dark images don't do well. Light images do well. 'Nuff said.

- **Sharpness is key** - Your photos should pop off the page. If they are blurry or unfocused, keep shooting until you have what you want.

- **Saturation over Desaturation** -

Saturation is just a fancy term for color intensity. And while you don't want to go overboard, opting for bright colors over desaturated grays that look like a Russian penal colony is always better.

- **White background (especially for product shots)** - This is hard to appreciate until you see your Pinterest image next to the rest of the Pinterest universe. But it can make a big difference to helping your pin stand out.

- **Simple is best** - Don't clutter your image with TOO many things, unless you're pinning an infographic. One subject for one pin image.

- **Things over faces** - This goes against most conventional thinking. But on Pinterest it's best to choose images of things, or abstract items, and less on human faces. (Could be because shots with faces often look like stock photos.)

- **Earth tones over ethereal tones** - I can't tell you WHY this is. But if your images have reds and oranges they will do exponentially better than images with blues and grays. (Not mine to question, only to do the bidding of the Color Gods.)

Perfect Pin Key No.4: Size Your Imagery

Just as important as what the image looks like is the sizing of the image.

Many people mistakenly believe there is only ONE top of image dimension you can use, the skyscraper "much taller than wider" type of image.

But this isn't true.

There are four types of images that work well on Pinterest:

- **The skyscraper** - This is the one you know and love. According to Pinterest the size that works best for this type of pin one that is 600 x 900 pixels or any photo in the 2:3 ratio.

- **The infographic** - Despite rumors to the contrary these still work. The key is to make sure your image is no bigger than 600 x 1260 pixels. (Otherwise Pinterest will crop your image and make it look strange.)

- **The Instagram portrait** - This plays well with Instagram. If you create an image in Instagram and want to repost on Pinterest — and why not? — then you'll automatically get a 600 x 750 pixels image you can use with great effect on Pinterest. Or you can custom-make an image in this portrait size.

- **The square** - People think square pins don't work. They do. You want to make sure you have an image that's 600 x 600 pixels, otherwise it'll look Pixelated.

Perfect Pin Key No.5: Write a Great Pin Description (and Tell People What You Want Them to Do)

It's in the description of your pin where the juicy marketing stuff happens.

There are SIX key elements to include in every pin description you write:

1. **A description of the what the hell people are looking at.** This should seem brain-dead obvious, but I'm shocked how many pins don't have a simple a caption telling us what we're looking at. (People are scrolling on their phone while they see your stuff. Don't make them think.)

2. **Keywords in body of text.** But not in an overdone, spammy sort of way. This will help people find your pins and boards in both the Pinterest search engine and external website search engines. (I generally

try to shoot for one keyword, two max.)

3. **A call-to-action** that tells people to either find out more about your product or service, opt-in to your email list or buy your product or service outright.

4. **An external link** for people to follow, based on the call-to-action you give them. Don't put in a shortened URL, such as http://bitly/375. These tend to be seen as spam. Put the entire link, including "http," in the description.

5. **One hashtag related to your specific business**. Such as #punkrockmarketing #discounttire #OldSpiceContest

6. **(Optional) The price of the product featured in the pin description.** This is done by typing the $ or £ in your description and adding the amount. (Pinterest will automatically add the price in a text overlay on the photo. Cool, huh?)

So, it would look something like this:

My newest Doctor Who themed steampunk jewelry piece! Check out our entire collection at: http:steampunkstuff.com #steampunkjewelry

I know some Pinterest gurus recommend you add TONS of #hashtags to your Pinterest description. You know, to help your pins get easily located in the Pinterest archives.

I don't advise this.

Adding a hashtag in your description simply gives people an invitation to leave your pin and check out a bunch of other people's stuff. (Pinterest users have a short enough attention span. I need not help it along any with some needless hashtags.)

Perfect Pin Key No.6: Share your Pin on Facebook and Twitter

You have a Facebook Page and Twitter account? Right?

Well, Pinterest makes it super simple to have your pins automatically show up as updates and tweets in your other social media platforms.

All you do is:

- Look under Pinterest settings
- Click on "Social Networks"
- Choose which social network you'd like Pinterest to share your activity with.

And yet, I'd like you to tread carefully with this.

The Twitter integration is fine, I ain't too worried about that. Twitter moves so fast, and there's so much stuff out there, that it's hardly worth worrying about.

But, with Facebook, it's possible to overload your fans. Studies have shown posting more than twice a day on a Facebook page suppresses engagement.

So instead, I recommend you add a Pinterest tab to your Facebook page. That way if people want to check out your "pins" they can do so there, but they won't feel overloaded with content.

To install the Pinterest app on your Facebook page, download and install the FREE WooBox Pinterest app.

All you gotta do is:

- Head over to WooBox.com
- Click "Get Started for Free"
- Sync the app up with your Facebook Page (You must be signed up to do this)

...and you're done! Su-per easy. (And it makes your Facebook page look a lot more filled out.)

Chapter 5 Key Takeaways:

- **Pinning success starts with finding great content to share.** (PopUrls, AllTop, Google Alerts and Photo-of-the-Day sites are perfect for this.)

- **Keep it visual.** Other good pieces of content to pin include: infographics, how-to stuff, product stills that don't suck, quote overlays on photos, and behind-the-scenes content.

- **Watch the clock.** The best time to pin SEEMS to be late afternoon, and after dinner. (Test to find the best time for you.)

- **Use the description wisely.** Include keywords, price points, and external links to your site in the description.

- **Promote your pins on Twitter and Facebook.** Set up the Twitter integration within the Pinterest dashboard, but create a Pinterest custom tab on your Facebook page to avoid fatiguing your Facebook fans.

Chapter 6:

7 Killer Strategies for Getting a Crapload of Pinterest Followers

"Why join the Navy if you can be a pirate?"
-Steve Jobs

All the pins and pinboards in the world won't do you much good if you don't have followers.

And that's what we will cover in this chapter: the subtle (and not-so-subtle) art of attracting Pinterest followers. (Who we can eventually turn into customers.)

In the next chapter I will show you how to make money from your Pinterest tribe. But for now, we gotta build the tribe before we can ask them to do things. (Like buy stuff from us!)

So, here are my SEVEN Top Tips for Finding a Collection of Rabid, Passionate (and Buying) Pinterest Followers:

Rabid Pinterest Tribe Tip No.1: Pin More Stuff

What? You mean I gotta pin…like…more stuff? 'Fraid so.

Pinterest rewards the dedicated, and slightly obsessed, with a ton of new followers. But those followers are like four-year-olds in a Chuck E. Cheese restaurant.

Very. Easily. Distracted.

That's why you got to keep the flow of pins, and pepperoni pizza, coming.

Research shows that the ideal pin sweet spot seems to be around 4-25 times a day.

Which sounds like a lot. (I know. Believe me.)

Until you realize it takes all of four seconds to pin something. (And if you've got the Pinterest bookmarklet added to your browser, less than that.)

The key thing is to come up with some kind of pinning routine that everybody on your team can follow.

This is the schedule I follow:

- **Noon** - Lunchtime: Three pins (1 promo pin, 2 cool stuff I found pins)
- **3:30 p.m.** - Afternoon break: Three repins
- **7:00 p.m.** - Evening pin session: Three pins (1 promo pin, 2 cool stuff I found pins)
- **10:00 p.m.** - Late-evening pin session: Three repins

Seriously, this takes me less than 10 minutes

total. Each day.

And by following this system I get myself 12 pins a day. Have other people on your team pitch in and before you know it your Pinterest pin total will be through the roof.

Rabid Pinterest Tribe Tip No.2: Repin Folks

This works the same as it does with Twitter. (Even more so.)

The fact is: after you repin somebody, they are likely to follow you back. (Most people are still NEW to Pinterest and having some kind of social interaction with people is cool.)

To keep it simple, I dedicate specific blocks of my pinning time to repinning. As my aforementioned schedule revealed, I focus my afternoon and evening sessions to repinning. (Which is good, because at those times all my brain cells can really handle is repinning.)

This does a couple of cool things.

If somebody is on their lunch break, and gets a smartphone notification I repinned them, they're **likely** to follow me.

And for the after-dinner session, early evening is prime Pinterest time, so I've got a great chance of adding that user to my tribe while they're amid some serious Pinterest activity.

But experiment. Find out what works for you.

Just make sure you devote time to repinning. (Your bank account will thank you.)

Rabid Pinterest Tribe Tip No.3: Follow Your Ideal Customers

This tip requires detective work. (And manual labor.)

But you want to put yourself in the mind of your ideal customer by asking:

- What type of boards would my ideal

customer follow?

- What keywords or phrases would they type into Pinterest?
- What are they looking for? (If your product or service fills a need or solves a problem, how would they find you?)

And then it's as simple as:

1. Type a keyword related to your ideal customer in the Pinterest search bar.
2. Choose the "Pinners" tab.
3. Start following "pinners" who share "pins" related to that keyword.
4. Follow approximately 50-100 people per "following" session.
5. Give 'em three days to follow you back. If they don't, unfollow them.
6. Rinse and repeat three times a week.

This is the same process I use to build my various Twitter tribes into the tens of thousands.

It's slow. It's monotonous. (And it totally

works.)

Rabid Pinterest Tribe Tip No. 4:
Follow the RIGHT Boards

This is exactly the same process as following "pinners." Only after you put your keyword in the Pinterest search bar, you choose "boards" instead of "pinners."

Give the creator of the board a couple of days to follow you back. If not, unfollow them. (Same as the pinner strategy: I like to do this three times a week, shooting for 20-30 new boards to follow each time.)

Rabid Pinterest Tribe Tip No.5:
Comment on Popular Pins

This is a super easy technique that a lot of Pinterest marketers neglect. All you do is:

- Head over to http://pinterest.com/popular.

- Find a couple of cool images that genuinely move you.

- Make a comment that doesn't suck.

You don't want to just say: "Cool share," "Agree," or "That's great."

Take time. Look at the image.

Read the description and make a halfway decent, meaningful comment. People love recognition, especially when it's sincere and heartfelt.

If you're stumped, just show you're passionate for the subject. (Even if you aren't.)

Rabid Pinterest Tribe Tip No.6: Find Your Friends

This only works if you have actual, human friends. If you're a hermit living in a cave in eastern Mongolia, this won't help.

Once you've connected your other social networks to your Pinterest account — we went over this in **Chapter 5** — you can easily look for those same friends and fans on Pinterest.

All you gotta do is:

1. Click on the name of your business account in the upper right-hand corner
2. Select "Find Friends"
3. Follow those "friends"
4. Wait for your Pinterest follower numbers to skyrocket

Rabid Pinterest Tribe Tip No.7: Run a Contest

Pinterest and contests go together like Lennon and McCartney. Simon and Garfunkel. Lady Gaga and...whatever weird outfit she's wearing these days.

Pinterest users LOVE contests. And they are a fan-tastic way to build your follower base FAST.

Which is why we're devoting an entire chapter to Pinterest contests in Chapter 8. (They're that awesome!)

Chapter 6 Key Takeaways:

- **Pin to win.** The more you pin, the more followers you'll get.

- **Repin to find followers.** People love recognition, and if you repin them they are likely to follow you back.

- **Find your ideal customer.** Use keywords in the Pinterest search bar and search for "pinners" who are pinning about areas related to your business.

- **Follow related boards.** Use the same "search" feature to find Pinterest boards that might contain folks who would make great followers for your account.

- **Hang with the popular kids.** Head over to pinterest.com/popular and comment on popular pins that are zooming up the Pinterest charts.

- **Find your friends (if you have some).** Use your Pinterest dashboard to connect with your existing social circle to broaden your Pinterest fan base.

Chapter 7:

7 Super-Ninja Ways to Make Money With Pinterest

"Nothing makes a man so adventurous as an empty pocket."

-Victor Hugo

Okay, we've gone over some traditional ways to incorporate Pinterest into your marketing arsenal. Create boards, pin stuff, sell your wares, buy yourself a yacht…

But there are real out-of-the-box ways you can

use Pinterest to kick-ass marketing effect.

And, trust me, your competition isn't doing any of these!

So, here are my SEVEN Super Ninja Ways to Use Pinterest That Nobody Knows About (But Now You Do):

Super-Ninja Pinterest Money-Making Tip No.1: Use Pinterest as Social Proof

Social proof is just a fancy phrase for using other people's positive opinions about a product or service to help future customers buy more of your stuff.

And it works really, really well.

If you've got an array of products for sale on your website, why not put a little button next to the products that are most popular on Pinterest?

That your organic eco-friendly baby diapers got 345 pins may not mean that much to you, but it means something to your customers.)

As consumers, we are always trying to compare

and judge things in our brain. That's why Amazon reviews and Consumer Reports ratings are so important. So make that job easier for your customers by putting a product's Pinterest popularity front and center.

Note: This works even better with a brick-and-mortar store where shop owners can put ACTUAL Pinterest stickers on price tags.

Super-Ninja Pinterest Money-Making Tip No.2: Have Customers Vote

The only thing people love more than sharing their opinion, is sharing that opinion when it counts for something.

One Pinterest technique that works really well is to display two products on your store's showroom floor or show pictures of two products on a dedicated website landing page, and have customers "vote" on their favorite, with the "winning" item being put on sale for some period.

Talk about consumer power.

Later on you can feature the winner in your store or on your website as a Pinterest bestseller. (You could even do a press release around the winner, with background on how you ran the contest. Journalists love behind-the-scenes stuff like that.)

And all of that interaction with your Pinterest account makes it much, much more likely that customers will eventually become Pinterest followers (And, hopefully, long-term customers.)

Super-Ninja Pinterest Money-Making Tip No.3: Create a Product Bundle Board

Folks love getting a deal. And there's nothing that feels quite like a killer deal than a product bundle.

If you've got a suite of products or services, then why not create a board that shows off these assets and offers a bundled price as well? (Say, if you were a flower company offering "wedding flower packages.")

All you do is set up a board with all your relevant products, and link each of the pins' descriptions to a landing page with a discounted bundle price.

And don't forget to promote this themed bundle on all your other social media platforms. A press release wouldn't hurt either.

Super-Ninja Pinterest Money-Making Tip No.4: Create a Client-Specific Board

Earlier we talked about creating a board that specifically recognizes a special client or board. But this tip takes that strategy much further.

What if you were a wedding planner? Would creating a client-specific board be a good idea?

Hell yeah!

Or what if you were a realtor? Would creating a client-specific board showing them photos of possible houses be a cool way to give them housing options?

I'd say so!

This may not be practical for everybody, especially those who sell low-ticket items.

But if you deal in any kind of sizeable margin items with your business, this would be a great way to offer your clients and customers a fantastic visual way to have their needs met.

And a reminder that you really care about them and don't see them as just customer automatons.

Super Ninja Pinterest Money-Making No.5: Run the Cheapest Focus Group Ever

Would knowing what your ideal customer wants, fears, and secretly desires be helpful to selling more stuff?

Uhh...yeah!

Well, skip the $500/hour consultant and run

your very own focus group.

Check out the boards of your followers and find out:

- What their passions are
- What super expensive merchandise they dream about owning
- What they want to look like
- What they feel is lacking in their life
- What kind of life they dream of having

And then collect all that data into a spreadsheet. (Interns, and teenage children, are perfect for this task.)

Once you have your data, brainstorm new products and services that solve these problems and connect with your customers on a deep and personal level. (Where all the real selling takes place.)

Super Ninja Pinterest Money-Making Tip No.6: Do What You Do Best

My grandfather had an expression: "Feed the stallions and starve the ponies."

And while my Grandad may not have been a contributor to the SPCA, the truth is he was right: you gotta exploit what's working and minimize what's not.

Nowhere is that truer than in your inbound marketing. And there's no better way to find what's working — and what's not — on your website than to discover which content from your website people are pinning.

To find this out, all you have to do is add your website into the following path:

Http://pinterest.com/source/yourwebsiteurl.com/ (Just to be crystal clear: you replace "yourwebsiteurl" with your own website. Don't want you wandering off into some weird corner of the Internet.)

This will give you a visual look at what's catching people's eyes. (And what's just sitting there like a mouse fart.)

Bonus: you might even come up with a couple of cool product ideas based on the content people are responding to.

Super Ninja Pinterest Money-Making Tip No.7: Show Off Your Team (and Your Expertise)

As any overpriced marketing guru will tell you, we buy from people we like.

Ever been to a bookstore and suddenly you come across that "Staff Picks" section? (You know the part of the store where over-qualified English majors share their literary faves?)

Suddenly you buy that depressing novel about Seattle oyster farmers in the 1890s because "Katie" the cashier said it "changed her life" and helped her appreciate the "moody, turbulence" of the Pacific

Northwest.

Without you realizing it, they've put a human face to their brick-and-mortar business and made you feel "connected." (And sold you crap you didn't want.)

So what better way to up the "like" quotient of your team than create a dedicated Team Pin Board where your staff can share:

- Cool things that inspire them
- Recent company outings
- The latest visually creative stuff they're working on
- Possible creative choices that followers could vote on (People love to feel included)

And you can also use this Pinterest real estate to:

- Call out a team member's recent accomplishment
- Brainstorm ideas for future products
- Share company logos (old and new)

Chapter Seven Key Takeaways:

- **Use testimonials.** Create a dedicated board where your customers and fans can gush about your products and services.

- **Let them vote.** Pit two of your products against each other to see what the Pinterest community likes best. (Be sure the winner goes on discount after the contest.)

- **Create a bundle board.** Organize your products and services into bundles you can place on a board and offer at a discounted group price.

- **Recognize your special clients.** Create a dedicated board for your best customers. (They'll love you for it.)

- **Run a focus group.** Do product research by poking around your ideal customers' boards and pins.

- **Find out what's working.** Check out what people are pinning from your site to discover the effectiveness of your content and potential product ideas.
- **Show off, but in a nice way.** Create a board that touts your team's accomplishments, passions, tastes and whatever else you like.

Chapter 8:

Pinterest Contests Made

Supremely Easy

"A business absolutely devoted to service will have only one worry about profits. They will be embarrassingly large."
-Henry Ford

Everyone loves to win FREE stuff. Everybody. And throw in the rather low barrier-to-entry of a Pinterest contest — you ain't asking people to write an essay, all they gotta do is upload a picture or create a board — and you've got the perfect marketing engine to attract tons of followers, boost your brand awareness and turn those freebie-seekers into paying customers who buy your wares.

But there's a new Pinterest sheriff in town.

And the old "Pin It to Win It" model of Pinterest contests is being phased out. Pinterest thinks these type of contests are spammy. (They're right.)

So, before we dig into the nuts-and-bolts of your Pinterest contest campaign let's go over what you CAN'T do:

- Require people to "pin" your contest guidelines. (Big no-no)
- Run a contest where pinners vote with likes, pins or repins.
- Require people pin a single image, or a selection of images, to enter the contest.
- Set up a contest where each follow, pin, or repin represents a single entry.
- Suggest that Pinterest endorses your contest.

Well, that kinda puts a crimp in things, don't it?

Don't worry.

All it did was kick the Internet hucksters out. (And leave room for us ethical marketers.)

So, here are my SIX tips for running a Pinterest contest that doesn't suck (and will actually make money):

Pinterest Contest Tip No.1: Set Your Goals

I know. Setting social media goals is about as much fun as filing a tax return.

But without a clear set of goals for your Pinterest contest — that you and your team understand beforehand — you'll be unsure of:

- How long to run the contest
- What kind of prize to offer
- How much money in advertising to put behind it... (Yes, it's possible you may have to spend money to spread the

word about your Pinterest contest. But it'll be worth it.)

Here are some of the more common Pinterest contest goals that marketers have used successfully:

- Increasing your number of Pinterest followers
- Finding more subscribers for your email list
- Promoting an upcoming product launch
- Getting publicity for your brand, product, service or cause
- Procuring feedback for…well…almost anything
- Boosting the amount of traffic to your website
- And…selling more stuff!

In my (not-so-humble) experience, the goals that I've had the most success with are getting more Pinterest followers, building up my email subscriber base and promoting a product launch.

I've had less success with getting "publicity" — whatever that means — and I find trying to simply sell more stuff hasn't worked out well for me.

But I don't move in the e-commerce space. If you sell physical products, you shouldn't have any problem.

And it's okay to have more than one goal with your Pinterest contest. But tread lightly…

Having more than two, maybe three, contest goals can water down your marketing efforts significantly. Don't worry, you can always run another contest next month to achieve different goals.

Pinterest Contest Tip No.2: Get Creative With Your Concept

This is where you get to flex your real marketing muscle. You just can't roll out the good-old "Pin It to Win It" contest model. It just means we need to be a little more creative, is all.

Here are a couple of contest concepts I've had REAL gains with:

- **Have users upload a photo or video of themselves** using your product or doing something related to your business.

- **Create a board** where users can come up with the most creative/interesting/funny/heartfelt idea for a specific project or topic. (People love to feel like they're part of your behind-the-scenes brainstorming.)

- **Have users "vote" on two prospective products or projects.** Make sure the winning product or project is offered on discount. And a couple of lucky winners get the item for free.

- **Have users create their OWN board around a theme** of your choosing. Carnival Cruise Lines had great success with this when they asked users to create four boards related to four different dream destinations. (If only their maintenance crew was as innovative.)

- **Have users FIND missing pieces of a pinboard puzzle**, somewhere on your website. Audi crushed this when they showed close-up images of a car and had people search their website for pictures that would fill in the rest of the automobile.

Pinterest Contest Tip No.3: Decide on the Rules

This is really just a matter of working out how long the contest is going to be (I recommend a week, no longer), what people need to do to win the contest and whether you are running a "sweepstake" or a "merit-based contest."

In case you're a little rusty on your contest terminology, a **sweepstake** is where somebody enters a contest and a winner is chosen at random.

A **merit-based contest** is where somebody performs an action, such as uploading a video or creating a board, and then the contest organizer picks the winner.

Both are great. Both work really well.

If you're running a sweepstake, you want to be careful you don't run afoul of Pinterest terms of service. (You can get all their info at: http://business.pinterest.com/brand-guidelines/)

As for what you should have entrants do, you could have them:

- Create boards
- Opt-in to your email list
- Follow your account
- Follow a specific board
- Upload a photo or video

I usually do a combination of things. Have them

FOLLOW me and enter their email address. (Or have them upload a photo or video.)

Just make sure you get some way to market to the entrants in the future. (Email is STILL my favorite way to go here.)

Pinterest Contest Tip No.4: Come Up With a Prize That Doesn't Suck

This will depend heavily on what type of business you have, and what kind of targeted lead you are trying to acquire.

Obviously if you're marketing to PR professionals than a one-hour coaching call might be something those folks would be into.

But if you're trying to reach a "non-marketing" population, then talking "marketing" for an hour may sound like government interrogation.

Just put yourself in your user's point of view. What would be cool to them?

- A one-year supply of Greek yogurt?

- A master bedroom set?

- A big-screen TV?

- A subscription to the Smithsonian Magazine?

- A candlelight dinner with Justin Bieber?

Whatever you do, keep the prize simple enough to understand that it can be explained in a single image.

A Victoria's Secret gift card is self-explanatory. (And in my wife's case... awesome.) A TCP/IP corporate network security firewall is not.

Pinterest Contest Tip No.5: Outsource the Anxiety

Right now, I'm going to share with you my secret weapon when it comes to Pinterest contests.

I handle none of it.

Really, most of the heavy lifting is done by an awesome, innovative company called Wishpond.

They are basically the go-to company for social

media contests and sweepstakes. I love Wishpond because their tools offer:

- Eye-catching imagery you can use to promote your contest.
- Custom entry forms. (Works great for email opt-in forms.)
- Sweepstakes compliance. (So you don't have to deal with any of the boring legal stuff.)
- Templates that make you look like an awesome web designer. (Even if you aren't.)
- The ability to "schedule" your contests in advance. (I've run contests while sitting on a beach in Oahu.)
- Landing-page templates that are mobile-friendly. (This is huge!)
- The ability to set up follow-up emails and customize entrant's messages to their friends.
- Killer analytics to let you know what's

working. (And what's not!)

- The ability to promote your contest on Twitter and Facebook really easily.

Sorry for the gushing **endorsement**. I like the services that Wishpond offers. Makes things SO MUCH easier.

And if you're extremely cheap, like I am, you can always run a 7-day contest within your two-week FREE trial and get all the benefit, with none of the cost.

Pinterest Contest Tip No.6: Promote the Contest Everywhere

Bit of an easy decision, this one. But it's still true. Promote your contest on:

- Twitter
- Facebook
- Instagram
- Your Blog

- YouTube
- Press Release
- Email Newsletter

…anywhere you can think of! (Again, if the prize is good, and the contest is creative, you WILL get a great response.)

And you may suddenly have thousands of new leads, for the price of a Victoria's Secret gift card.

Chapter Eight Key Takeaways:

- **Come up with contest goals first.** Are you going after new followers, new email subscribers...or simply trying to get press attention? Decide on goals, then come up with your strategy.

- **Go beyond the usual.** Come up with a creative concept that asks people to do MORE than just create a board or pin an item from your website.

- **Lay down the law.** Come up with the rules of your contest. (And make sure, if it's a sweepstake, you follow Pinterest terms of service.)

- **Find a quality prize.** Bonus points if it fits in with the area of your company's expertise.

- **Let somebody else handle the contest.** Choose a tool like Wishpond to handle all the tech-y stuff associated with your contest.

- **Promote!** Spread the word about your contest on your blog, Twitter feed, YouTube Channel, Facebook page…anywhere you can think of.

Chapter 9: Standing on the Shoulders of (Pinterest) Giants

"The mind is not a vessel to be filled, but a fire to be kindled."

-Plutarch

WORDS can only do so much.

I've tried to share some of the tips and tricks I've learned (the hard way) about how to turn all those pins and repins and boards of the Pinterest universe into actual money.

But sometimes, you just gotta SEE it.

So, in this final chapter, I will share with you some companies I think are doing a GREAT job on Pinterest, and in particular, what area of Pinterest I think they are killing it in.

Don't be intimidated if some of them are big brands and huge companies. There are plenty of big companies who suck at Pinterest, if they have any Pinterest presence at all.

Just collect ideas you can use for your own Pinterest marketing efforts, and before you know it, you might be one of the big guys yourself.

Pinterest All-Star No.1: Chobani Greek Yogurt

The company that made Greek yogurt a national food phenomenon knows what it's doing with Pinterest.

Not only do they have boards that extoll the many benefits of Greek yogurt — it's healthy for you ("Fit With It" board), it's great baked ("Baked With Chobani"), it's awesome frozen ("Chilly Chobani") — but they also do a fantastic job of recognizing their fans ("Chobani Champions") and creating little nuggets of inspiration that have nothing to do with yogurt ("Nothing But Good" and "Go Real").

All-Star Resource: http://pinterest.com/chobani

Pinterest All-Star No.2: Etsy

Etsy, that handcraft marketplace that rejuvenated more craft rooms in America than the glue gun, was practically made for Pinterest and its visual revolution.

Of course, Etsy has plenty of themed boards that show off their awesome wares — ("Etsy Jewelry," "Cool Spaces", "DIY Projects") — but they also utilize the guest contributor feature quite well, with their series of "Guest Pinner" boards.

Also, the "Etsy Kids" and "Etsy Weddings" boards show this company ain't just about buying cool, handmade stuff made in a rural Pennsylvania farmhouse.

It's about being creative and teaching the next

generation that not everything should be made in a factory overseas.

All-Star Resource:http://pinterest.com/etsy

Pinterest All-Star No.3: Gap

The company who can't seem to decide on a logo they want, actually has a pretty good Pinterest strategy in place.

They don't have a ton of boards, but the ones they do have do a lot more than just show off the latest back-to-school styles.

Gap does a great job of getting their followers to post pictures of themselves wearing Gap clothing ("Styld.by You") and they've also created a clever board, called "GAPgrams," where users put their Gap outfits together in anthropomorphic poses...and then share them on Instagram. (Sounds weird, but it totally works.)

Note: Notice how many of their product photos have a white background...not a coincidence.

All-Star Resource: http://pinterest.com/gap

Pinterest All-Star No.4: Whole Foods Market

They call it food porn for a reason. But the Whole Foods Pinterest page offers a lot more than pretty pictures of soy burgers and seaweed grass smoothies.

It also offers fitness and nutrition tips for kids ("Kids: MOVE That Body," "A LunchBox That's Tops"), creative holiday boards ("Creative Christmas Projects"; "Spring Gatherings"), information on the company itself ("#WhyAustin") and the most popular of all, a board that allows followers to express their thanks for the role food plays in their life ("#foodthanks").

I'm not sure what I think about them putting their logo on NEARLY every pin, but overall it's a good brand to emulate.

All-Star Resource:

http://www.pinterest.com/wholefoods/

A Final Note

If the Internet is still in its infancy. Then Pinterest is in its first trimester.

It's still not clear how the whole business model will shake out for Pinterest.

- Will external websites get pissed off Pinterest is monopolizing their traffic? (Flickr sure is mad. Wonder who's next?)
- Will Pinterest charge users?
- Will they push paid placement like Facebook, Twitter and Instagram have?

What we know, due to its overwhelmingly quick rise up the social media charts, is that Pinterest has hit a NERVE.

And that **nerve** is all about photos and videos that inspire and motivate people.

So, as you dip your toe into the Pinterest marketing waters, remember though the tactics of this super-trendy social network may change...

The strategy is here to stay.

- Keep it visual.
- Keep it simple.
- Keep it positive.

I have real doubts that people will actively read long-form text on a screen in the future. (And as an English major, that mortally offends me.)

But the more you can present the story of your company in a simple, compelling image...

...the more your business will be poised to not just **survive** these crazy, chaotic economic times.

But thrive. (And what could be more inspiring and motivating than that.)

Here's hoping YOU thrive and kick some

serious ass in your Pinterest efforts.

If you have any questions or comments drop me a line at michael@punkrockmarketing.com.

And if you've enjoyed this book, or even if you didn't enjoy the book, would you be willing to leave a review?

Even a sentence or two really helps us indie authors carve out a career as a creative professional.

HEAD OVER to PunkRockMarketing.com/PinBook to leave a review on Amazon (and enjoy truckloads of good karma):

Oh, and just one more thing…

A Special FREE Gift for You!

If you'd like FREE instant access to my seminar "How to Make a Damn Good Living With Social Media (Even If You Hate Social Media" then head over to **PunkRockMarketing.com/Free**. (What else you gonna do? Watch another "Twilight" movie?!)

DISCLAIMER AND/OR LEGAL NOTICES:
Every effort has been made to accurately represent this book and it's potential. Results vary with every individual, and your results may or may not be different from those depicted. No promises, guarantees or warranties, whether stated or implied, have been made that you will produce any specific result from this book. Your efforts are individual and unique, and may vary from those shown. Your success depends on your efforts, background and motivation.

The material in this publication is provided for educational and informational purposes only and is not intended as business advice. Use of the programs, advice, and information contained in this book is at the sole choice and risk of the reader.

Made in the USA
Middletown, DE
02 August 2019